Yun and the Giant Bird

Chapter		Page
1	Bird Attack	2
2	Yun's Chance	8
3	The Dragon King	14
4	The Magic Feather	18

Written by Charlotte Raby

Illustrated by Simona Sanfilippo

Chapter 1
Bird Attack

Yun was walking in the mountains when he saw something very strange. He saw a huge crowd of people running away from a village.

"What's going on?" thought Yun. Was another adventure about to start?

When they saw Yun, the villagers shouted to him, "Run! Hide! A giant bird is attacking our village!"

Yun looked up and saw the giant bird. It shrieked and flapped across the sky.

"Don't worry," said Yun to the villagers. "I can help you. I will scare the giant bird away!"

The villagers were very surprised. How could this young boy scare a giant bird?

Chapter 2
Yun's Chance

Yun went into the village. Food from the market stalls rolled on the ground. Tables and chairs lay smashed in the street. The roofs of the houses had been torn apart.

Yun crept silently through the streets, keeping a sharp look-out for the giant bird.

Suddenly, a huge beak snapped at him. Yun yelped with fear and ran into a shop to hide. But the shop had no roof, and a huge, dark eye peered down at him!

Yun thought quickly. He grabbed some silk and ran out of the shop.

Yun rubbed his dragon charm to use the power of flight. He glided up into the sky above the village, and the giant bird flew after him. Yun started to fly in circles around the giant bird. He wrapped the silk around the bird. The villagers watched, amazed!

Chapter 3
The Dragon King

Just as Yun thought he had won, the bird snipped at the silk. With a shriek, it flew away.

"I need help," Yun groaned. He rubbed his dragon charm and called the Dragon King.

The Dragon King came quickly.

"Have you found out why the bird is here?" he asked.

"No!" said Yun. "I just want to scare it away."

"I think you need to talk to it," the Dragon King replied.

Shaking with fear, Yun went back to find the giant bird. It was waiting for him.

"Why have you come back, little boy?" the bird asked.

"To find out why you are here," replied Yun.

The bird was amazed.

"No one has ever asked me *why* before. They just fight me. So I will tell you."

Chapter 4
The Magic Feather

Yun and the giant bird talked all night.

The next day, they went to see the villagers.

"This is Peng," Yun told them. "She wants to build a nest, but cannot find a place. So she tried to build a nest in the village. She knows this is wrong now. Can we help her?"

The villagers were very pleased to hear that Peng did not want to harm them.

"Of course we can help!" said a young woman. The other villagers nodded. They found Peng a good place to build her nest, in the forest near the village.

Later, Peng and her chicks looked down at Yun from their nest in the forest.

Peng gave Yun one of her feathers.

"Give this to the villagers," she said. "It is a magic feather. If they ever need me, I will come."

So Yun presented the feather to the villagers. Then he went to see the Dragon King and the princess.

"You have been brave and kind," said the old man.

The Dragon King blew on Yun's dragon charm and it shone brightly. At once, Yun changed into a dazzling, blue dragon.

"You can change whenever you wish now," said the Dragon King. "Your adventures show you have the heart and courage of a dragon."